Contents

Enterprise and entrepreneurship 1
    Key concepts in dynamic business activity 1
    Types of economic sectors 1
    New business ideas 1
    Risk and reward in business activity 2
    The role of entrepreneurship 2

Business opportunities 3
    Customer needs 3
    Market research 3
    Market segmentation 4
    Competition 4

Business objectives 5
    Business aims and objectives 5
    Changing business aims and objectives 5
    Revenues, costs, and profits 5
    Cash and cash flow 6
    Sources of business finance 6
    Limited and unlimited liability 6
    Factors influencing business location 6
    Types of business ownership 7

    The marketing mix (4Ps) 8
    Business plans 8
    Businesses success and failure 8
    Methods of business growth and their impact 9
    Sources of finance for growing businesses 9
    Measuring business size 9
    Impact of globalisation on businesses 10
    Barriers to international trade 10
    How businesses compete internationally 10
    Multinational companies (MNCs) 10
    Ethical considerations in business activity 11
    Pressure groups 11
    Environmental concerns in business activity 11

Influences on businesses 12
    Stakeholders 12
    The business cycle 12
    External factors and adaptability 12
    Technology 13
    Evaluating technology's influence on business 13
    Legislation 14
    Consumer law 14
    Employment law 14
    Economic climate 14

Contents

Marketing **15**
- Product – the design mix and product life cycle 15
- Price – pricing strategies and influences 15
- Promotion – marketing to different segments 15
- Place – distribution methods 15
- Integrated marketing mix for competitive advantage . 15
- Mass markets vs. niche markets 16
- Legal controls on marketing 16

Operations **17**
- Purpose of operations 17
- Technology in production 17
- Economies and diseconomies of scale 17
- Managing stock 18
- Procurement and supply 18
- Quality in goods and services 19
- The sales process and customer service 19
- Sustainable production methods 19

Finance **20**
- The need for business finance 20
- Using quantitative data for business decisions 20
- Gross profit and net profit 20
- Profit margins and average rate of return (ARR) . . . 21
- Statement of financial position (Balance Sheet) . . . 21
- Profitability ratios 21
- Liquidity 21

Human resources **22**
- Function of human resources 22
- Organisational structures 22
- Leadership styles 22
- Ways of working 23
- The impact of technology on working arrangements . 23
- Job roles and responsibilities 24
- Effective communication 24
- Types of recruitment 25
- Key recruitment documents 25
- Stages in the recruitment process 25
- Employment contracts and legal controls 26
- Trade unions 26
- Downsizing and redundancy 26
- Training and development 27
- Motivation in the workplace 27

Formula sheet **28**

Enterprise and entrepreneurship

Key concepts in dynamic business activity

Businesses must constantly adapt to survive and grow. The business environment is 'dynamic' because it's influenced by ongoing changes in technology, consumer preferences, and market conditions. New business ideas emerge either from fresh thinking or by modifying existing products.

- Business activity involves producing goods and services to satisfy customer needs and wants. The purposes of a business are to:
  - Produce goods and services
  - Meet customer needs
  - Add value by converting inputs (resources) into outputs (products/services)
- **Factors of production:**
  - **Land:** natural resources used in production (e.g. farmland, oil, timber).
  - **Labour:** human effort (mental and physical) used in production (e.g. teachers, factory workers, hairdressers).
  - **Capital:** man-made resources used in production (e.g. machinery, buildings).
  - **Enterprise:** the entrepreneur who organises the other three factors and takes risks (e.g. business owners, start-up companies).
- **Adding value:** is the difference between the **selling price** and the **cost of inputs**. This is how businesses make profit and differentiate their product. Ways to increase added value include:
  - **Branding** e.g. Apple products sold at premium prices.
  - **Quality** e.g. handmade artisanal chocolate vs mass-produced
  - **Convenience** e.g. Uber/Deliveroo's door-to-door service
  - **Design** e.g. brands like Dyson or John Lewis known for sleek stylishness
  - **Unique Selling Point (USP)** e.g. Innocent's ethical, humorous marketing of their drinks
- **Opportunity cost:** is the **benefit lost from the next best alternative** when a choice is made. For example: choosing to buy stock for a new product means you can't invest in marketing, so the lost marketing impact is the opportunity cost.

Types of economic sectors

Businesses operate in **three sectors of the economy**, each producing different types of goods/services.

Sector	Description	Examples
Primary	Extracts natural resources	Farming, fishing, mining
Secondary	Manufactures goods from raw materials	Car production, construction
Tertiary	Provides services	Retail, education, healthcare

Businesses can also be in either the private or public sector.

Sector	Description	Examples
Private	Owned by individuals or companies to make profit	Tesco, BP, ASOS
Public	Owned and run by governments to provide essential services	NHS, police, public schools

New business ideas

Business ideas arise due to changes in the business environment.
- **Changes in technology:** new tech leads to new products/services. For example: developments in AI have led to products like ChatGPT.
- **Changes in what consumers want:** tastes and preferences change over time. For example: increased focus on sustainability has led to more demand for plastic-free products and electric vehicles.
- **Products becoming obsolete:** older products become less useful or outdated. For example: DVDs have been replaced by streaming, and landline phones have been replaced by mobile phones.
- New business ideas come from:
- **Original ideas:** innovative solutions to new or existing problems, often based on identifying a gap in the market. For example, Airbnb disrupted the traditional hotel industry.
- **Adapting existing products/services:** improving, rebranding, or finding new uses. For example, Uber offers a variety of options (e.g. XL, Lux, Comfort, Green) to meet different customer needs.

Enterprise and entrepreneurship

Risk and reward in business activity

Entrepreneurs weigh **risks** against potential **rewards** before starting a business. Every business decision carries risk, especially for entrepreneurs starting a new venture. However, these risks can bring significant rewards if the business succeeds. Understanding the balance between risk and reward is essential for good decision-making.

Risks	Description	Example
Business failure	Poor planning, low sales, or competition causes closure	Poundland in the UK closing many stores, struggling to compete with online discount retailers like Temu
Financial loss	Losing money personally or via loans/investments	Toys R Us went out of business in 2018 with £15 million in unpaid taxes
Lack of security	No guaranteed income, pension, or job benefits	Company founders often will not earn a substantial salary until their business achieves financial stability

Rewards	Description	Example
Business success	Building a well-known, growing business	Gymshark became a £1bn+ company in under 10 years using influencer marketing
Profit	Financial gain from added value	Canva was founded in 2012 and now has an annual revenue of US$3 billion
Independence	Being your own boss; control over decisions	Innocent smoothies initially run as a side business by university graduates

The role of entrepreneurship

All specs except: Pearson IGCSE

An **entrepreneur** is someone who
- Organises resources (land, labour, capital)
- Takes the financial risk
- Makes business decisions

Characteristics of successful entrepreneurs:

Trait	Description
Risk-taker	Willing to take calculated risks
Determined	Doesn't give up easily
Innovative	Finds creative solutions
Hardworking	Puts in long hours and effort
Resilient	Can recover from setbacks

Governments support entrepreneurial start-ups because they:
- Create jobs
- Drive innovation
- Increase tax revenue
- Boost the economy

Method	Example
Grants	Financial help without repayment
Low-cost loans	Government-backed loans with low interest
Training schemes	Business bootcamps and mentorships
Advice services	Enterprise agencies, online resources

Business opportunities

Customer needs

Understanding customer needs is vital for a business to succeed. These needs are the expectations customers have when buying a product or service. If businesses fail to meet these, they risk losing sales and customers to competitors.

- **Customer needs** refer to the essential factors customers look for when buying a product or service. This includes:
  - **Price:** affordable and competitive pricing; products must match what customers are willing to pay (e.g. ALDI offering cheaper groceries).
  - **Quality:** customers expect good durability, reliability, and satisfaction, especially at higher prices (e.g. Apple iPhones)
  - **Choice:** variety of options, features, customisation (e.g. ASOS with wide clothing selection, or tiered subscription models)
  - **Convenience:** ease of access and use (e.g. apps, Click & Collect)
- Importance of understanding customers:
  - Helps to generate **sales** by meeting expectations
  - Essential for **survival**, especially in competitive markets
  - Enables **loyalty** and repeat customers
  - Better understanding = **better targeting and satisfaction**
  - Happy customers return and recommend the business, leading to **long-term reputation and stability**

Market research

Market research helps businesses make informed decisions based on data, not guesswork. It involves gathering, analysing, and interpreting information about customers, competitors, and the market.

- **Purposes of market research:**
  - Identify and understand customer needs
  - Spot gaps in the market
  - Reduce risks
  - Inform business decisions (pricing, product design, marketing)
- **Role of social media in market research:**
  - Quick, real-time insights into trends and opinions.
  - Platforms like Instagram and TikTok show what's popular.
  - Businesses track hashtags, reviews, mentions, etc.

- **Methods of market research:**
  - **Primary research:** based on data collected first-hand through surveys, focus groups, or observation.

Method	Advantages	Disadvantages
Survey	Collects specific data quickly	Can be biased; may have low response rate
Questionnaire	Easy to analyse if structured well	Poorly worded questions reduce validity
Focus group	In-depth insights	Small scale; not always representative
Observation	Real-world behaviour	No customer opinions; limited insight

  - **Secondary research:** uses existing data such as government reports, statistics, online resources, and databases.

Source	Advantages	Disadvantages
Internet	Fast, wide range of info	May be inaccurate or outdated
Market reports	Professional, reliable	Often expensive
Government reports	Accurate, detailed, freely available	May not be specific to niche markets

- **Importance of reliable data:**
  - Data must be accurate and up to date.
  - Unreliable data leads to poor decisions and wasted money.

Types of data in market research	Description	Example
Qualitative	Opinions and reasons (why people behave)	"Why do you prefer this brand?"
Quantitative	Numbers/statistics (what people do)	"70% of customers buy coffee before 9 a.m."

Business opportunities

Market segmentation

Market segmentation divides a broad market into smaller groups that share common characteristics.

- **Types of market segmentation:**

Segment type	Explanation	Example
Location	Geographical region	Ice cream vans operating in crowded areas during summer
Demographics	Age, gender, education, etc.	Cosmetics aimed at teenage girls
Lifestyle	Hobbies, interests, values	Elite sports gear for fitness enthusiasts
Income	Economic bracket	Budget supermarkets vs. luxury retailers
Age	Generational preferences	Social media platforms for Gen Z vs. Boomers

- **Market mapping:** a diagram showing how products/brands are positioned in the market. This helps identify **gaps in the market** and **competitor positioning.** For instance, below is a market mapping of UK supermarkets (approximate positions for example purposes).

Competition

All businesses operate in a competitive environment unless they are a monopoly. Understanding competition helps a business to differentiate and succeed.

- **Competitor strengths and weaknesses:**

Factor	Strength example	Weakness example
Price	High prices can signal high status or high quality	High prices may drive away any customers who can't afford them
Quality	Premium products earn more customer satisfaction	Cheaply made goods may be unreliable
Location	Having many outlets or a dominant online presence increases visibility	Stores may have low footfall and be expensive to continue operating
Product range	A wide selection increases the chance of having something for everyone	Niche stores may lack variety and struggle to reach the right audience
Customer service	Personalised and efficient service helps brand reputation and positive customer sentiment	Poor service can lead to bad reviews, directly impacting the business' reputation and chance to acquire new customers

- **Impact of competition on business decisions:** competition can encourage efficiency, innovation, and customer focus as businesses may need to:
  ◦ Lower prices
  ◦ Improve product quality
  ◦ Innovate faster
  ◦ Focus on customer service
  ◦ Offer promotions

Business objectives

Business aims and objectives

All businesses need direction. Aims describe the overall goal and objectives break the aim down into measurable targets. These differ depending on the type and size of the business, and whether it's new or established.

- **Financial aims:**
  - **Survival:** main aim for startups and during crises.
  - **Profit:** used for growth, rewards, or reinvestment.
  - **Sales:** targets to increase market presence.
  - **Market share:** beat rivals and gain influence.
  - **Financial security:** steady cash flow and long-term stability.
- **Non-financial aims:**
  - **Social objectives:** helping society (e.g. B Corporations).
  - **Personal satisfaction:** fulfilment from doing what you love.
  - **Challenge:** personal growth, testing limits.
  - **Independence:** control over working life and direction.
- **Aims may differ due to** business size, ownership type, owner priorities, and what stage of the business lifecycle the business is in.

Changing business aims and objectives

As businesses grow and respond to their environment, their aims and objectives often evolve. This is normal and reflects changing priorities and external pressures.

- **Why aims and objectives change:**
  - **Market conditions:** a recession may force a shift from growth to survival.
  - **Technology:** new tech may create new opportunities (e.g. AI tools).
  - **Performance:** a strong performance may encourage expansion.
  - **Legislation:** new laws may require ethical/environmental adjustments.
  - **Internal factors:** changes in leadership, ownership, or staff.
- **How aims and objectives change**
  - **Start-up stage:** focus on survival and breaking even.
  - **Growth stage:** increase profit and expand market share.
  - **Maturity:** improve efficiency, innovate, or reduce costs.
  - **Decline or recovery:** exit markets, reduce workforce, or rebrand.

Revenues, costs, and profits

Understanding money flow is key to success. Businesses track revenue, costs, and profit to make decisions. Profits can be reinvested, while losses can lead to changes or closure.

- Key terms:
  - Revenue = Price × Quantity Sold
  - Fixed Costs: do not change with output (e.g. rent).
  - Variable Costs: rise as output increases (e.g. ingredients).
  - Total Costs = Fixed Costs + Variable Costs
  - Profit = Revenue − Total Costs
  - Loss: when costs > revenue.
  - Interest = (Total Repayment − Borrowed) ÷ Borrowed × 100
  - Break-even: sales needed to cover all costs.
  - Margin of Safety = Actual Sales − Break-even Sales
- Break-even diagram:

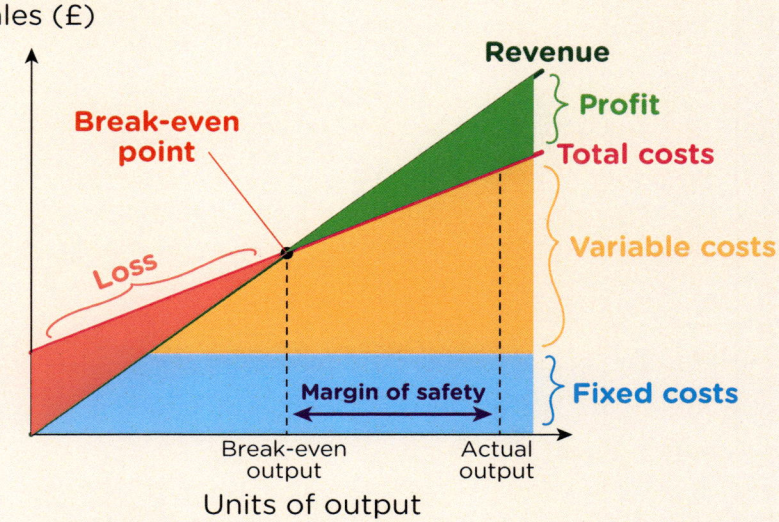

  - **Break-even point**: where no profit or loss occurs. Higher costs mean the break-even point increases, whereas lower price means the business needs to sell more.
  - **Profit area**: where revenue exceeds costs.

Business objectives

Cash and cash flow

Cash is the lifeblood of a business. Even profitable businesses can fail if they run out of cash to pay bills. Cash flow forecasting helps anticipate problems and plan accordingly.
- Why cash matters:
  - Paying suppliers, employees, and rent
  - Avoiding insolvency
  - Maintaining operations during tough months
- **Cash ≠ Profit.** Profit is calculated over time, whereas cash is about timing of inflows/outflows. A business can be profitable but cash-poor.
- **Forecasting cash flow:**
  - **Inflows:** sales revenue, loans, investments.
  - **Outflows:** salaries, stock, bills.
  - **Net cash flow = Inflows – Outflows**
  - **Opening balance:** cash at start of period.
  - **Closing balance = Opening + Net Cash Flow**

Sources of business finance

Businesses need funding to start, grow, and operate. The right source depends on the purpose, amount, cost, and length of time the money is needed. Finance is divided into short-term (day-to-day needs) and long-term (growth, equipment).
- **Short-term sources:**
  - **Overdraft:** flexible but costly if used long.
  - **Trade credit:** 'buy now, pay later' – needs good supplier trust.
- **Long-term sources:**
  - **Personal savings:** owner's own money – risky but interest-free.
  - **Venture capital:** investors provide money and advice for equity.
  - **Share capital:** selling shares; only for limited companies.
  - **Loans:** borrowed from banks and repaid with interest.
  - **Retained profit:** internal source from past profits.
  - **Crowdfunding:** many small investors via platforms like Kickstarter.

Limited and unlimited liability

All specs except: CIE

Liability means legal responsibility for business debts and actions. The amount of liability a business owner has depends on the type of ownership.
- **Limited liability:** the owner's financial risk is limited to the amount invested in the business. Personal assets are protected; only business assets can be used to pay debts. This is common in private limited companies.
- **Unlimited liability:** the owner is personally responsible for all business debts. Personal assets (like a house or car) can be used to pay off business debts. This is common in sole traders and partnerships.
- For example, if a sole trader bakery goes bankrupt with £20,000 debt, the owner may need to sell personal belongings. In a private limited company, the owner's liability is limited to their investment in shares.

Factors influencing business location

Location choice affects operating costs and access to customers.

Factor	Why it matters
Proximity to market	Being close to customers can increase convenience and sales.
Proximity to labour	Access to skilled or affordable workers is crucial.
Proximity to materials	Lowers transport costs, especially for manufacturers.
Proximity to competitors	Depends on the industry: good for restaurants (cluster effect), bad for monopolies.

Impact of the internet on location:
- E-commerce allows businesses to operate from remote or cheaper locations.
- Online-only businesses (e.g. ASOS, Amazon) reduce costs by not needing physical shops.
- Businesses may still need fixed premises for warehousing, customer service, or branding, but this is more flexible as they are not dependent on foot traffic and the proximity factors above.

Business objectives

Types of business ownership

Businesses can choose different legal structures depending on their needs, risk tolerance, and growth plans.

- **Sole trader:** one individual owns and runs the business (e.g. a freelance graphic designer or local hairdresser).

Advantages	Disadvantages
Easy to set up	Unlimited liability
Keeps all profits	Harder to raise finance
Full control over decisions	Business may stop if the owner is ill or dies

- **Partnership:** two or more people share ownership, responsibilities, and profits (e.g. an accountancy or law firm)

Advantages	Disadvantages
Easier access to capital than sole traders	Unlimited liability for all partners
Shared workload and responsibilities	Disagreements can occur
Shared skills and ideas	Profits must be shared

- **Private Limited Company (Ltd):** a business owned by shareholders, typically family or close associates. Shares are not sold to the public (e.g. Gymshark started as a Ltd before growing into a global brand).

Advantages	Disadvantages
Limited liability for shareholders	More complex and costly to set up
Easier to raise finance through share sales	Legal paperwork and regulations to follow
Continuity if owner leaves or dies	Accounts are public (less privacy)

- **Public Limited Company (PLC):** as businesses grow, they may become PLCs – companies that sell shares on the stock market (e.g. Tesco).

Advantages	Disadvantages
Raise large amounts of capital	Complex and costly to set up
Shares can be traded publicly	Subject to strict regulations
Enhanced public image	Takeover risk from hostile shareholders

- **Franchises:** when a business (franchisor) allows someone else (franchisee) to trade using its brand, business model, and support. For example, McDonald's is one of the most recognised global franchises.

	Advantages	Disadvantages
For the franchisor	Rapid expansion	Less control over day-to-day operations
	Regular income through franchise fees	Poor franchisee performance affects brand
For the franchisee	Lower risk using an established brand	Initial fees and ongoing royalty payments
	Support with training and marketing	Limited freedom to make decisions

- **Joint ventures:** two or more businesses agree to work together on a specific project (e.g. Google and NASA collaborating to create Google Earth).

Advantages	Disadvantages
Shared risks and resources	Profits must be shared
Access to new markets or customers	Different business cultures can clash
Combined expertise and capital	Decision-making can be slow or complex

- **Social enterprises:** businesses that aim to make a profit but reinvest most of it into social or environmental causes (e.g. The Big Issue magazine sold by people experiencing homelessness).

Advantages	Disadvantages
Addresses social issues	Can struggle to raise capital
Builds community trust	Profit-making may be limited
Often supported by government grants	Less attractive to some investors

Business objectives

The marketing mix (4Ps)

The **marketing mix** is the combination of four key decisions businesses make to meet customer needs and compete effectively.
- The 4Ps of the marketing mix are:
    - **Product:** the goods or services sold (quality, features, design).
    - **Price:** how much customers are charged (subject to pricing strategies).
    - **Place:** where and how the product is sold (online, in-store) via its distribution channels (wholesalers, retailers, or direct to consumers).
    - **Promotion:** advertising and communication (social media, billboards, discounts).
- **How the elements work together:**
    - A premium product must be priced high and promoted as luxury.
    - A budget product may rely on low price, high availability, and simple packaging.
    - All 4Ps must align to target a specific customer group.
- **Impact of changing consumer needs:** as trends change, businesses must adjust the 4Ps:
    - New product designs to meet ethical or environmental demands.
    - Adjusted prices during inflation.
    - Switching promotion to social media if targeting Gen Z.
- **Technology and the marketing mix:**
    - **E-commerce**: 24/7 availability, wider reach, lower overheads.
    - **Digital communication:** social media marketing, targeted ads, email campaigns.

Promotion
- Public relations
- Social media
- Channels
- Ads

Price
- Price strategy
- Financing
- Discounts
- Payment terms

Product
- Features
- Quality
- Branding
- Customer service

Place
- Locations
- Logistics
- Transport
- Market coverage

Business plans

A business plan is a written document that outlines what a business does and what it aims to achieve. It helps entrepreneurs clarify their ideas and make strategic decisions before launching. A business plan is often needed by banks or investors to assess the risk of lending money.
- A business plan typically includes:
    - **Business idea:** the product or service and what problem it solves.
    - **Aims and objectives:** what the business hopes to achieve.
    - **Target market:** who the customers are, backed by market research.
    - **Revenue, cost, and profit forecast:** financial predictions showing viability and profitability.
    - **Cash-flow forecast:** estimates of cash inflows and outflows to avoid running out of cash.
    - **Sources of finance:** where funding will come from (e.g. loans, investors).
    - **Location:** why a specific place was chosen and the facilities required.
    - **Marketing mix:** the 4 Ps.
- **Purpose of planning business activity:**
    - Planning reduces **risk** by forcing entrepreneurs to consider what could go wrong. A clear plan improves the chances of securing **finance**, as lenders want to see how funds will be used.
    - For example, a start-up café that prepares a detailed plan (with realistic revenue and location analysis) is more likely to attract investment than one with vague ideas.
    - It helps set **measurable objectives** so progress can be monitored.
    - Encourages **long-term thinking**, not just short-term survival.

Businesses success and failure

Success factors	Failure factors
Strong management	Poor planning or leadership
Unique product or innovation	Lack of market research
Good cash-flow management	Running out of cash
Access to funding	High debt levels or loan rejection
Meeting customer needs effectively	Ignoring competition or changing trends
Adapting to change (in tech, economic conditions)	Failure to adapt (e.g. Blockbuster vs Netflix)

Business objectives

Methods of business growth and their impact

As businesses become established, they often aim to grow to increase revenue, market share, and influence. Growth can happen **internally** (organically) or **externally** (inorganically).

- **Internal (organic) growth:** happens when a business expands using its own resources, without merging or taking over another firm.
  - **New products:** developing new goods or services via innovation or R&D to attract more customers (e.g. Apple continues to grow through constant product development like AirPods or Vision Pro).
  - **New markets:** entering new geographic locations or customer segments.
  - **Changing the marketing mix:** adjusting the 4Ps to boost sales.
  - **Online expansion:** using e-commerce to sell to more people without opening physical stores.
- **External (inorganic) growth:** involves joining with other businesses, either by **merging** or **taking over**:
  - **Merger:** two businesses agree to join together to form one larger business.
  - **Takeover:** one business buys another (can be hostile or agreed).
- **Integration:**
  - **Horizontal:** merging with a competitor (e.g. two clothing retailers).
  - **Vertical forward:** buying a customer in the supply chain (e.g. manufacturer buys retailer).
  - **Vertical backward:** buying a supplier (e.g. bakery buys wheat farm).

Method	Advantages	Disadvantages
Organic growth	Low risk, builds on strengths	Slow, limited by internal resources
Mergers	Share skills, grow quickly	Risk of conflict or culture clash
Takeovers	Instant access to market or assets	Expensive, risk of redundancy or resistance
Horizontal integration	Reduces competition, increases market share	Regulatory scrutiny, loss of diversity
Vertical integration	Control supply chain, improve margins	Costly, may lack expertise in new stage

Sources of finance for growing businesses

Source	Internal/External	Description
Retained profit	Internal	Profit kept in the business for reinvestment
Selling assets	Internal	Selling unused equipment, buildings, etc.
Loan capital	External	Borrowing money from a bank, with interest
Share capital	External	Selling shares to investors (Ltd or PLC)
Market flotation	External	Public can buy shares on the stock market

Measuring business size

Measuring business size helps track growth and compare with competitors. However, no single method is perfect.

- **Methods of measuring business size:**
  - **Number of employees:** total staff numbers.
  - **Value of output/sales:** total income from goods/services sold.
  - **Volume of output/sales:** quantity of products made or sold.
  - **Capital employed:** total value of money invested in the business.
- Note that **profit** is **not** a valid measure of size (a small firm can be more profitable than a large one).
- **Problems measuring size:** some businesses operate on low margins but high volume (e.g. supermarkets), different sectors have different capital needs (e.g. finance vs farming).

Reason for growth	Explanation
Owner's ambition	Desire for more income, status, or challenge
Economies of scale	Reduced costs through bulk buying or automation
Access to finance	Larger businesses can borrow more easily
Market demand	Growing industries drive business expansion

Reason for staying small	Explanation
Lifestyle choice	Owner prefers flexibility and control
Lack of capital	No access to funding to expand
Niche market	Only serves a small, specialised audience
Avoiding complexity	Growth brings legal and HR responsibilities

Business objectives

Impact of globalisation on businesses

Globalisation refers to the growing interconnectedness of businesses and economies across the world. It allows companies to operate internationally, access new markets, reduce costs, and grow rapidly, but it also brings challenges such as increased competition and ethical concerns.

- **Imports:** when a business buys goods or services from another country.
  - Allows access to cheaper or higher-quality materials and products.
  - Can increase competition from foreign firms that offer lower prices.
  - For example, British retailers importing electronics from China to reduce costs.
- **Exports:** selling goods or services to customers abroad.
  - Helps UK businesses expand their market and increase revenue.
  - May require changes in packaging, pricing, or marketing to suit foreign customers.
  - For example, Burberry exports high-end fashion to Europe, the US, and Asia.
- **Changing business locations:**
  - Businesses may move operations (e.g. manufacturing) abroad to reduce costs.
  - This can lead to job losses in the home country but may lower prices for customers.
  - For example, Dyson moved its vacuum cleaner production to Malaysia to cut costs.

Barriers to international trade

- **Tariffs:** taxes imposed on imported goods to make them more expensive than local products.
- **Trade blocs:** groups of countries that agree to remove trade barriers between members.
  - Examples of trade blocs include the European Union (EU), North American Free Trade Agreement (NAFTA), and Association of Southeast Asian Nations (ASEAN).
  - Trade blocs make it easier to trade within the group but can complicate trade with countries outside.
  - Brexit led to the UK leaving the EU trade bloc, introducing new barriers for British exporters.

How businesses compete internationally

- **Using the internet and e-commerce:**
  - Businesses can reach global customers through websites and digital platforms.
  - E-commerce reduces the need for physical stores in each country.
  - For example, ASOS sells fashion globally through its online store.
- **Changing the marketing mix (4Ps):**
  - **Changing product:** tailoring to local tastes, laws, or climates (e.g seasonal menu items at fast food chains).
  - **Changing price:** adjusted based on local incomes, taxes, or tariffs.
  - **Changing place:** moving or acquiring locations based on access to customers.
  - **Changing promotion:** translating and localising advertising; may require cultural sensitivity for specific international markets.

Multinational companies (MNCs)

- **Multinationals (MNCs):** large businesses that operate in more than one country (e.g. Coca-Cola, McDonald's, Unilever, and Shell). They often have offices, factories, or sales teams across continents.
- **Advantages of becoming an MNC:**
  - Access to international markets in a host country increases customer base and sales.
  - Reduced costs through access to cheaper labour and raw materials.
  - Spread business risks across different regions.
  - Economies of scale through larger-scale operations.

Advantages for host countries	Disadvantages for the host countries
Jobs: MNCs often provide employment in local factories or offices	**Environmental damage:** MNCs may pollute or overuse natural resources
Investment: may build infrastructure (e.g. factories, roads, tech facilities)	**Exploitation:** may pay low wages or provide poor working conditions
Increased choice: consumers benefit from wider product range	**Competition:** local businesses might be outcompeted by large MNCs
Economic growth: may boost exports and GDP for the host country	**Repatriation of profits:** MNCs often send profits back to the home country rather than reinvesting locally

Business objectives

Ethical considerations in business activity

Ethics in business is about doing what is morally right, not just what is legal or profitable. Ethical businesses consider the impact of their actions on workers, customers, communities, and the environment.

- Ethical businesses will:
  - Avoid exploiting workers or suppliers
  - Refuse to test on animals or use unsustainable materials
  - Pay fair wages and avoid child labour
- Being ethical can increase brand loyalty, but it may also increase costs.
- For example, Fairtrade brands pay higher prices to farmers to ensure ethical supply chains.
- **Trade-off between ethics and profit:**

Ethical choice	Impact on profit
Paying fair wages	Higher wage bills may reduce short-term profits
Eco-friendly packaging	Sustainable materials may cost more
Avoiding cheap labour	Production costs increase without outsourcing to low-cost countries

Pressure groups

- **Pressure groups:** are organisations that try to influence business or government decisions (e.g. Greenpeace, Extinction Rebellion). They can target unethical business practices through protests, social media, or campaigns.
- For example, pressure from environmental groups led Coca-Cola to reduce its use of single-use plastics and increase bottle recycling schemes.
- **How pressure groups affect the marketing mix:**

Marketing mix	Possible Impact
Product	Businesses may remove harmful/unethical ingredients
Price	May increase due to more expensive ethical sourcing
Promotion	Ensure truthful advertising about sustainability claims
Place	Pressure to reduce reliance on long-distance transport

Environmental concerns in business activity

- Businesses are under pressure to reduce their environmental impact.
- Eco-friendly actions include things like using renewable energy in factories, reducing packaging or using recyclable materials, and offsetting carbon emissions by planting trees.
- For example Patagonia spends more on sustainable materials, but gains loyal customers who value its ethics.
- **Trade-off between environment and profit:**

Environmental choice	Impact on profit
Environmentally friendly policies	Build brand trust and attract eco-conscious consumers, but may be costly in the short-term
Sustainable materials instead of cheaper conventional materials	Sustainable materials are often more expensive initially, but reduce environmental harm, landfill waste, and carbon footprint
Investing in renewable energy or energy-efficient equipment	High upfront costs (e.g. solar panels, electric vehicles) but lower carbon emissions and utility bills, though the business may not see a return on investment for several years

- **Why businesses respond to environmental issues:**
  - Improve brand reputation and appeal to ethical consumers.
  - Gain a competitive advantage in eco-friendly markets.
  - Comply with legal requirements or avoid penalties.
  - Meet the expectations of investors or partners who value sustainability.
  - For example, IKEA has invested in renewable energy and aims to become fully circular (zero waste) by 2030.
- **How business activity can harm the environment:**
  - Pollution (air, water, noise) from factories, vehicles, and waste.
  - Overuse of non-renewable resources like oil and minerals.
  - Deforestation or destruction of wildlife habitats.
  - For example, fast fashion brands contribute to water pollution and landfill.
- **How businesses may respond to environmental issues:**

Response	Explanation
Energy efficiency	Using LED lighting, solar panels, or better insulation
Green supply chains	Sourcing materials locally or from eco-certified suppliers
Waste reduction	Reusing packaging, recycling materials
Product innovation	Creating biodegradable or recyclable products

Influences on businesses

Stakeholders

A **stakeholder** is anyone who has an interest in the activities and performance of a business. Different stakeholder groups often have different (and sometimes conflicting) objectives.

- Key stakeholders and their primary objectives are:
  - **Shareholders (owners):** want high profits and return on investment (dividends).
  - **Employees:** seek job security, fair pay, and good working conditions.
  - **Customers:** expect good-quality products/services at reasonable prices.
  - **Managers:** want success for the business and career progression.
  - **Suppliers:** prefer regular orders and prompt payments.
  - **Local community:** wants jobs and minimal environmental disruption.
  - **Pressure groups:** try to influence business activity to support ethical or environmental issues.
  - **Government:** interested in businesses paying taxes and providing employment.
- **How stakeholders are affected by businesses:**
  - Employees may be made redundant during cost-cutting.
  - Customers are affected by pricing and quality decisions.
  - Suppliers depend on businesses for income.
- **How stakeholders influence business activity:**
  - Shareholders can vote out directors.
  - Customers can stop buying products.
  - Pressure groups may create negative publicity.
- **Conflicts between stakeholders:**

Conflict	Example
Shareholders vs. Employees	Shareholders want to reduce costs; employees want higher wages
Customers vs. Shareholders	Customers want lower prices; shareholders want higher profits
Managers vs. Local community	Managers may want to build a new site; locals may object to noise or traffic

The business cycle

The **business cycle** refers to the economic environment in which businesses operate. It has four main stages – **growth, boom, recession,** and **slump** – and affects demand, employment, and business investment.

Stage	Description	Impact on business
Growth	Economy recovers, GDP rises	Sales increase, investment grows
Boom	Peak of economic activity	High demand, high prices, full employment
Recession	GDP falls, demand falls	Sales drop, job losses, cost-cutting
Slump	Prolonged low activity	Businesses may close, high unemployment

- **Economic indicators and effects:**
  - **Employment:** high employment means more consumer spending, whereas unemployment reduces demand for goods/services.
  - **Inflation:** rising prices may increase costs and reduce customer spending. Stable inflation helps businesses plan ahead.
  - **Economic growth:** strong growth creates opportunities for expansion, whereas a shrinking economy can reduce confidence and profits.

External factors and adaptability

- Businesses do not operate in isolation. **External factors** like economic conditions, new laws, or changes in technology can affect how they perform and compete, provided they adapt to these changes.

External factor	Business response example
Technology	Invest in automation, launch an app/social media strategy
Legislation	Revise contracts, train employees, improve workplace safety
Economic climate	Change pricing, shift focus to value products, delay expansion

- Why adaptability matters:
  - Being flexible allows businesses to survive and thrive during change.
  - Firms that monitor external factors (e.g. through market research or trend analysis) can make informed decisions.
  - Adapting quickly can lead to competitive advantage, especially in fast-moving sectors like retail or tech.

Influences on businesses

Technology

Technology transforms how businesses operate, sell, and communicate. It brings both opportunities and challenges.

- **Sales:** technology allows businesses to grow their customer base and improve how they sell products and services. It opens up new sales channels, enhances customer experience, and increases availability.
  - **Online platforms** (e.g. websites, apps, marketplaces like Amazon or Etsy) allow businesses to reach customers globally, 24 hours a day, 7 days a week. This removes the limitations of physical opening hours and location. For example, a small skincare start-up in Manchester can sell to customers in Singapore or Canada using an e-commerce website, using tools like Shopify to easily create user-friendly sites.
  - **Social media** (e.g. Instagram, TikTok, Facebook) enables businesses to:
    - Promote products directly to users through targeted ads.
    - Engage with followers through comments, streams, or influencers.
    - Turn platforms into mini sales platforms. For example, Instagram allows product tagging with direct links to purchase pages.
  - **Customer data collection** (e.g. cookies, CRM systems) helps businesses by tracking browsing and buying habits, recommending products, and personalising email marketing and promotions.
- **Costs:** technology can both increase and decrease business costs. It often involves large upfront investment, but brings long-term efficiency.
  - **Automation and robotics** can significantly reduce **labour costs**, particularly in manufacturing or repetitive service roles. Over time, automation can reduce wage bills and human error. However, it may also require technical maintenance and lead to job losses.
  - **IT systems and software** (e.g. inventory management, accounting software, analytics) help reduce administrative costs and human error. For example, Xero or QuickBooks can automatically track business income and expenses, reducing the need for an in-house accountant. While this saves money in the long term, the software itself can be expensive upfront.
  - **Cloud computing** (e.g. Google Drive, Microsoft OneDrive) lowers hardware costs by letting businesses store data online instead of on physical servers. This reduces office space and energy use, but may require monthly subscription fees and cybersecurity investments.
- **Marketing mix:** technology reshapes all elements of the marketing mix:
  - **Product:** dfaster product development through prototyping tools like 3D printing or virtual design, or customisation (e.g. Nike By You trainers).
  - **Price:** price comparison websites (e.g. CompareTheMarket, Skyscanner) make it easy for consumers to find cheaper alternatives. Businesses may have to lower prices or use dynamic pricing (e.g. airlines, ride-sharing apps).
  - **Promotion:** Google Ads and social media campaigns allow small businesses to compete with larger ones. However, this is an area of ongoing legislative concern and subject to government regulation. E-newsletters and email campaigns offer personalised promotions and reminders, helping businesses build customer loyalty. Viral marketing and influencer campaigns can also increase reach at a low cost.
  - **Place:** e-commerce reduces or removes the need for physical retail space. Businesses save on rent, utilities, and staffing, and customers shop from home, improving convenience. Furthermore, click-and-collect and home delivery combine digital convenience with local service. Supermarkets like Tesco offer apps that let customers order online and collect at the store.

Evaluating technology's influence on business

Area	Positive impacts	Potential challenges
Sales	Reach wider audiences, 24/7	Greater global competition
Costs	Low labour costs, higher efficiency	High upfront investment, training needed
Product	Easier customisation, e.g. software updates	Customer expectations for innovation rise
Price	Data-led pricing; dynamic pricing	Transparent pricing forces competitiveness
Promotion	Targeted ads, lower costs, viral campaigns	Can be ignored or blocked by users
Place	Reduced overheads, global access	Logistics complexity; cybersecurity risks

Influences on businesses

Legislation

Legislation refers to the **laws and regulations that govern how businesses operate**. These laws aim to **protect stakeholders**, including **consumers**, **employees**, and the **general public**. Legislation covers a wide range of business areas such as product safety, working conditions, employee rights, advertising, and pricing.

- **Why legislation matters for business:** businesses must **comply with legal requirements** or face serious consequences, including:
  - **Financial penalties** (fines, legal costs, compensation)
  - **Reputational damage** and thus a loss of customers or employees
  - In serious cases, **criminal charges** for directors or business owners
- Legislation helps ensure businesses act **responsibly, ethically, and fairly**, and **levels the playing field** with minimum standards for all businesses.

Impacts of legislation	Description
Increased costs	Compliance may require staff training, legal advice, better facilities, or safety equipment.
Avoid penalties	Following the law avoids fines, lawsuits, and business shutdowns.
Improved reputation	Ethical businesses attract loyal customers and top talent. Being known for fairness and safety can be a unique selling point.

Consumer law

All specs except: Pearson IGCSE

Consumer protection laws ensure that people buying goods and services are **treated fairly** and have **basic rights** when things go wrong. The UK's **Consumer Rights Act 2015** states that products and services must be:

- **Of satisfactory quality:** the product should meet the standard that a reasonable person would expect, considering price and description.
- **Fit for purpose:** the product must work for the intended purpose or any purpose made known to the seller.
- **As described:** the product must match its description, packaging, or advertising. Misleading claims are illegal.
- **Consumer rights** include the right to a **full refund** within 30 days if a product is faulty, the right to **repair or replacement** if a fault occurs after 30 days, and the right to **reject digital content** that does not work.

Employment law

Employment law protects workers and governs how businesses recruit, pay, and treat staff. Major UK laws include the **Equality Act 2010**, the **Health and Safety at Work Act 1974**, and the **National Minimum Wage Act 1998**.

- **Recruitment:** must be fair and non-discriminatory. Employers cannot reject applicants based on **protected characteristics** such as age, race, gender, disability, religion, or sexual orientation.
- **Pay:** employers must pay at least the **National Minimum Wage** (or National Living Wage, depending on age). Failing to meet this requirement can result in heavy fines and public "naming and shaming."
- **Health and safety:** businesses must provide a safe working environment, including risk assessments, safety equipment, and training. For example, a factory must provide ear protection if noise exceeds legal limits.
- **Anti-discrimination:** all employees must be treated equally. Discrimination during recruitment, promotion, pay, or dismissal is illegal.

Economic climate

The economic climate includes factors like inflation, interest rates, unemployment, and changes in consumer income. A strong economy leads to **higher consumer spending**, **business growth**, and **job creation**. A weak economy may cause **reductions in demand**, **layoffs**, or **reduced investment**.

Factor	Impact on businesses
Unemployment	High unemployment = lower disposable income → reduced demand for non-essentials.
Consumer income	Higher incomes = more discretionary spending. Lower incomes = demand for value brands.
Inflation	Rising input costs (e.g. raw materials, wages). Businesses may raise prices or cut costs.
Interest rates	High rates make borrowing more expensive (affects investment). Low rates encourage borrowing and spending.
Taxation	Higher taxes reduce consumer spending power and business profits. Lower taxes boost demand and investment.
Exchange rates	A **weaker pound** makes UK exports cheaper abroad (good for exporters) but imports more expensive. A **stronger pound** has the opposite effect.

Marketing

Product – the design mix and product life cycle

Marketing involves understanding customer needs and creating a strategic mix of product, price, promotion, and place (the **4Ps**) to deliver value, build brand, and support competitive advantage.

- The **design mix** refers to balancing **function**, **aesthetics**, and **cost** when designing a product.
  - **Function:** the product must work as intended (e.g. a smartphone that connects reliably).
  - **Aesthetics:** appeal and style matter (e.g. Apple iPhones are sleek and visually attractive).
  - **Cost:** production costs must be kept low to maintain profitability.
- The **product life cycle** describes the stages a product goes through:
  1. **Introduction:** product launch with low sales and high costs.
  2. **Growth:** sales rise rapidly, profits start increasing.
  3. **Maturity:** sales peak; intense competition; prices may fall.
  4. **Decline:** sales drop as consumers move on.

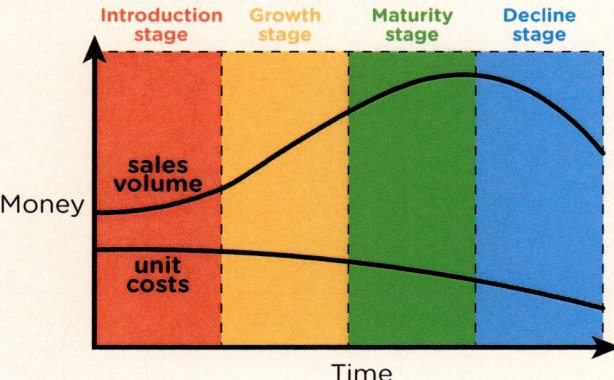

- **Extension strategies** can prolong the maturity stage and delay decline:
  - Updating the product (e.g. new iPhone features).
  - Reducing price to attract price-sensitive buyers.
  - Finding new market segments (e.g. subscriptions, accessories).
- **Differentiation** is important because it helps a business stand out from competitors. For example, Dyson vacuums differentiate through advanced technology and design. Differentiation may be based on quality, service, branding, or unique features.

Price – pricing strategies and influences

- Common pricing strategies:
  - **Penetration pricing:** low initial price to gain market share.
  - **Price skimming:** high launch price for innovations or new versions.
  - **Competitive pricing:** matching or slightly undercutting competitors.
  - **Cost-plus pricing:** adding a markup to unit cost.
  - **Psychological pricing:** setting price at £9.99 to seem cheaper.
- Factors influencing pricing strategies:
  - **Technology:** online tools allow dynamic pricing (e.g. airline tickets).
  - **Competition:** high competition may force lower prices.
  - **Market segments:** premium markets can accept higher prices.
  - **Product life cycle:** prices may drop during maturity/decline stages.

Promotion – marketing to different segments

- Promotion strategies include: **advertising** (TV, print, online ads), **sponsorship events, influencers**, **product trials**, **special offers** (e.g. discounts, coupons or buy-one-get-one), and **branding** (creating a clear, recognisable brand identity).
- Use of **technology** in promotion:
  - **Targeted advertising online:** ads appear based on user data.
  - **Viral/social media campaigns**: e.g. #ShareACoke, TikTok challenges.
  - **E-newsletters:** email campaigns tailored to customer preferences.

Place – distribution methods

- **Place decisions** involve choosing channels to make products accessible to the appropriate customers at the right time.
- Businesses distribute via **retailers** (i.e. physical stores like Boots or Tesco) and **e-tailers** (online-only platforms like Amazon or ASOS).

Integrated marketing mix for competitive advantage

- Each element of the marketing mix influences the others: a low-cost product (price) needs low-cost design and production (product), while innovative products may need premium branding (promotion) and selective outlets (place).
- An **integrated marketing mix** uses all 4Ps coherently to build a **competitive advantage**. For example, Starbucks offers high-quality coffee (product), premium pricing (price), strong branding (promotion), and convenient locations and delivery options (place).

Marketing

Mass markets vs. niche markets

Understanding the distinction between **mass markets** and **niche markets** is essential for analysing how businesses position their products, make marketing decisions, and manage risk.

- **Mass markets:** are large markets that target the general population with **standardised products** that have broad appeal. Products in mass markets are typically found in supermarkets or mainstream retail outlets and include items like toothpaste, smartphones, or soft drinks.

Advantages of mass markets	Disadvantages of mass markets
Large sales volume: mass markets offer the potential to sell in high volumes, which increases revenue and supports brand recognition.	**High competition:** many firms compete for the same broad audience, making it hard to differentiate.
Economies of scale: large-scale production and distribution lower the average cost per unit, improving profit margins. This allows businesses to invest more in marketing and innovation while maintaining competitive pricing.	**Changing consumer preferences:** a shift in public opinion or trends (e.g. towards healthier lifestyles) can dramatically affect demand for mass-market products like sugary drinks.
Brand dominance: successful brands in mass markets can gain significant market share and become household names.	**Lower profit margins:** price competition is fierce, which can drive down profit margins.

- **Niche markets:** target a smaller, specific group of customers with products tailored to their unique preferences, lifestyles, or values. These products are not aimed at the general public and often involve customisation or exclusivity.

Advantages of niche markets	Disadvantages of niche markets
Premium pricing: niche products often justify higher prices because they address unique needs.	**Smaller market size:** fewer potential customers means lower total revenue, especially if the product is specialised.
Strong customer loyalty: targeting a specific group allows for deep brand connection, resulting in repeat purchases and positive word-of-mouth.	**Limitations on growth:** there may be a low ceiling on potential customers and thus minimal opportunities to expand the business.
Clear market positioning: easier to establish a distinct identity compared to mass markets.	**Risk of changing trends:** if customer tastes shift, the business may quickly become irrelevant.

Legal controls on marketing

Marketing is a powerful business tool, but it must be **ethical and lawful**. In the UK, several legal controls exist to ensure that businesses promote their goods and services **honestly and responsibly**. These rules are enforced by organisations like the **Advertising Standards Authority (ASA)**.

- **Purpose of legal controls:** the main aim is to protect consumers from:
  - **False or misleading promotion**: This includes exaggerated claims, omitted information, or fake endorsements that could deceive customers. For example, a skincare product that claims to "cure acne overnight" without scientific proof would be in breach the law.
  - **Faulty goods:** products must meet safety and quality standards. Marketing cannot disguise defects or poor performance.
- Laws that support this in the UK include:
  - **Consumer Protection from Unfair Trading Regulations 2008** – bans misleading advertising and aggressive sales tactics.
  - **Consumer Rights Act 2015** – ensures product quality, as discussed previously.
  - **Trade Descriptions Act 1968** (now mostly absorbed into other laws) – requires all descriptions of products or services to be accurate and not misleading.
- **Effects of legal controls on businesses:**

Effect	Description
Accurate advertising required	Businesses must fact-check claims, verify components, and avoid exaggeration
Compliance costs	Legal compliance may involve consulting lawyers, training staff, and reviewing campaigns
Avoiding penalties	Non-compliance can lead to fines, bans on advertising, or legal action
Protecting brand image	Ethical marketing enhances a company's reputation, especially amongst socially conscious customers
Product development pressure	Firms may need to adjust packaging, testing, or materials to meet legal standards before advertising or launching products

Operations

Purpose of operations

Operations is the area of business concerned with producing goods or delivering services efficiently and at the right quality. Effective operations reduce costs, improve productivity, and support customer satisfaction.

- **Purpose of operations:**
  - To **produce goods** or **provide services** that satisfy customer needs.
  - To maintain **quality**, control costs, and manage resources effectively.
  - To support continuous improvement and efficiency.
- **Production processes:**
  - Types of production:
    - **Job production:** making one-off, customised products (e.g. bespoke furniture).
    - **Batch production:** producing a set number of identical items before switching (e.g. a bakery making batches of buns).
    - **Flow production (mass production):** continuous production on assembly lines (e.g. car manufacturing).
  - Impacts of these processes:
    - Job production allows high customisation but is slow and costly.
    - Batch production balances flexibility and efficiency.
    - Flow production achieves high productivity and low unit cost but is inflexible.

Technology in production

Technology impacts business operations via:
- **Automation and mechanisation** (e.g. robotic arms in car factories).
- **Computer-Aided Manufacture (CAM):** precision manufacturing from digital designs.
- **3D printing:** rapid prototyping and bespoke components.

Advantages of technology for business operations	Disadvantages of technology for business operations
Lower labour costs and higher output	High initial investment in systems and equipment
Improved consistency and quality control	Job losses or retraining required for workers

Economies and diseconomies of scale

As businesses grow, they often benefit from **economies of scale** which are cost advantages gained when output increases. However, if they grow too large, they may face **diseconomies of scale**, which increase per-unit costs due to inefficiencies.

Economies of scale (lower unit costs with growth)		
Type	Description	Example
Purchasing	Buying in bulk reduces unit costs	Supermarkets securing discounts from suppliers
Marketing	Spread advertising costs over more units	A national TV ad reaching millions of customers
Financial	Larger firms often access cheaper credit	Banks offering lower interest to established firms
Managerial	Specialised managers boost productivity	A finance director managing budgets more efficiently
Technical	Investment in machinery reduces per-unit costs	Automated bottling lines at Coca-Cola plants

Diseconomies of scale (rising unit costs from overgrowth)	
Issue	Description
Communication problems	Large organisations may suffer from unclear or delayed communication across departments.
Motivation and loyalty	Employees may feel disconnected or undervalued in large, impersonal structures.
Coordination inefficiencies	Managing large operations can become slow and bureaucratic, reducing agility and increasing costs.

Operations

Managing stock

Stock (or inventory) refers to the raw materials, work-in-progress, and finished goods held by a business. Managing stock effectively is critical for **ensuring smooth production, minimising costs**, and **meeting customer demand**. There are two primary tools used in stock management: bar gate stock graphs, and the just-in-time approach.

- **Bar gate stock graphs:** a visual way of showing how stock levels change over time. For example, a bakery might use a bar-gate graph to ensure flour is reordered before stock levels fall below the minimum, avoiding disruption to daily operations. These graphs help businesses determine:
  - **Minimum stock level:** the lowest amount of stock that should be kept on hand.
  - **Maximum stock level:** the highest level to avoid overstocking.
  - **Reorder level:** the point at which new stock should be ordered to avoid running out.
  - **Lead time:** the time between placing an order and receiving the stock.

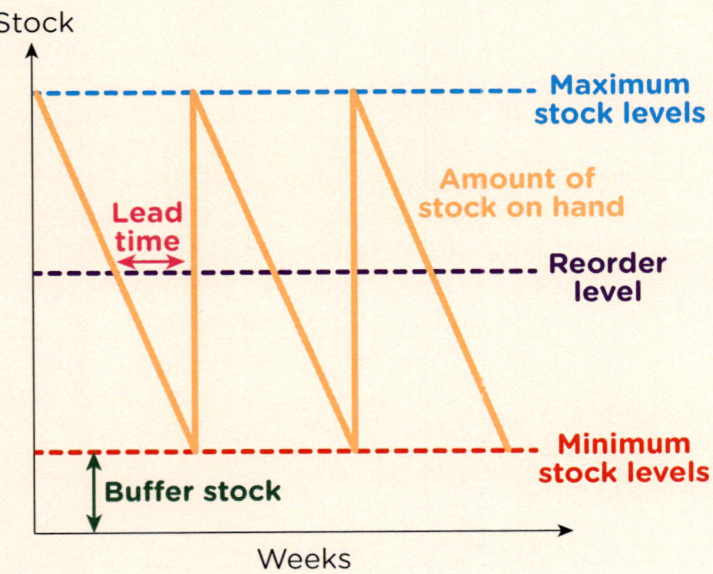

- **Just-in-Time (JIT) stock control:** is a **lean stock management strategy** where materials are ordered and received only when needed for production or sale. This method aims to **reduce storage costs** and **avoid excess inventory**.

Advantages of JIT	Disadvantages of JIT
Lower storage costs: no need to maintain large warehouses.	**High dependency on suppliers:** delays or disruptions in the supply chain can halt production.
Less wastage: perishable goods or obsolete stock are less likely to be wasted.	**No buffer stock:** unexpected demand or supplier issues can lead to stockouts.
Improved cash flow: capital isn't tied up in unused inventory.	**No ability to limit disruption:** delays in any one part of the system leave the entire production chain vulnerable.

Procurement and supply

Procurement is the process of selecting suppliers and purchasing the goods and services a business needs to operate. Effective procurement balances **cost, quality, and reliability**.

- **Key procurement factors:**
  - **Quality:** poor-quality materials and defects damage reputation.
  - **Delivery:** timely and reliable delivery avoids production delays.
  - **Cost:** competitive pricing improves profitability.
  - **Trust:** good supplier relationships encourage flexibility and reliability.
- **Impact of logistics and supply chain decisions:**

Area	Impact
Costs	Faster shipping (e.g. air freight) is more expensive but may be necessary for perishable or urgent goods.
Customer satisfaction	Late deliveries or stockouts damage customer trust.
Reputation	Ethical sourcing and smooth logistics build a brand's credibility.

Operations

Quality in goods and services

Delivering consistent **quality** is essential to business success. Poor quality leads to dissatisfied customers, returns, and damage to brand image.
- Methods of quality management:
  - **Quality control (QC):** inspecting products after production to catch defects. This is **reactive** meaning it responds to problems when they arise. For example, mobile phone companies will conduct QC checks on the finished devices for screen or component issues before packaging them for sale.
  - **Quality assurance (QA):** building processes that ensure quality at every stage. This is proactive because it predicts and prevents issues from arising. This includes things like staff training, process checks, and inputting quality standards.
- Why quality matters:
  - **Customer loyalty:** satisfied customers are more likely to return and recommend the business.
  - **Cost reduction:** fewer returns mean lower operational costs.
  - **Competitive edge:** high-quality products can justify premium pricing and attract more customers (e.g. Apple is known for rigorous quality assurance in hardware and software, so maintains premium pricing).

The sales process and customer service

A strong sales process and excellent customer service are key to generating revenue and building long-term relationships.
- The steps in the sales process are:
  1. **Product knowledge:** sales staff should understand features, benefits, and potential concerns.
  2. **Efficient service:** fast, friendly service creates positive experiences.
  3. **Customer engagement:** responding to questions/feedback builds trust.
  4. **After-sales service:** includes warranties, returns, customer support.

Why customer service matters:
- **Loyalty and retention:** repeat customers mean more stability.
- **Positive reviews and reputation**: word-of-mouth is powerful marketing.
- **Premium pricing:** good service justifies higher prices as added value.

Sustainable production methods

Sustainability in business refers to **minimising negative environmental impacts** while maintaining profitability and social responsibility. Increasingly, consumers expect companies to take meaningful environmental action.
- **Sustainable methods include:**
  - **Renewable energy:** solar, wind, and hydroelectric sources reduce reliance on fossil fuels.
  - **Waste minimisation:** recycling materials, reducing packaging, and using biodegradable resources.
  - **Eco-friendly products:** designing goods that are recyclable, reusable, or made from sustainable materials. For example, the clothing company Patagonia uses recycled fabrics and runs clothing repair programs to reduce waste, boosting customer loyalty.

Advantages of sustainable production methods	Disadvantages of sustainable production methods
Enhanced reputation: companies are seen as ethical and forward-thinking.	**High initial costs:** upgrading machinery or switching to sustainable materials can be expensive.
Cost savings: over time, reduced waste and energy use can lower costs.	**Complex changes:** supply chains may need restructuring, and staff need retraining.
Attracting conscious consumers: more customers actively choose green businesses.	**Zero sum costs:** the business may be better off spending money elsewhere to make a bigger impact

Finance

The need for business finance

Finance is at the heart of every business operation for both short-term needs and long-term investments, including paying for resources, staff, and innovation. To achieve its objectives, businesses must know where money is coming from, how it is managed, how financial performance is measured, and how financial information supports business decision-making.

- **Start-up capital:** buying initial equipment, premises, inventory, and technology. For example, a new bakery needs ovens, counters, and an initial stock of ingredients.
- **Expansion:** opening new branches, hiring more staff, or entering new markets. For example, a fast food chain may open in another city.
- **Asset replacement:** upgrading outdated machinery or vehicles. For example, manufacturing companies regularly need to replace the equipment they use to ensure effective and efficient operations.
- **Investment in technology:** automating processes or developing digital tools. For example, lots of clothing retailers have mobile apps to facilitate online shopping and incentivise customer loyalty.
- **Working capital:** the money needed for daily operations.
  - Working Capital = Current Assets – Current Liabilities
  - A healthy working capital level ensures the business can operate smoothly. For example, a florist might receive payments from customers upon delivering bouquets, but needs to pay suppliers upfront for flowers.

Using quantitative data for business decisions

Businesses use data to make informed decisions and identify trends. This helps compare profit margins across product lines and can forecast the impact of pricing changes.

- Types of data:
  - **Financial:** income statements, cash flow forecasts.
  - **Marketing:** sales figures, customer surveys.
  - **Market:** competitor analysis, economic indicators.
- Limitations of data:
  - **Lag:** data may be outdated by the time it's used.
  - **Incomplete:** not all factors are captured.
  - **Qualitative factors:** doesn't show customer loyalty, staff morale, etc.

Gross profit and net profit

Profit is the surplus money after subtracting costs from income. It is key to evaluating a business's financial health.

The **Statement of Profit and Loss** is a document summarises revenues and expenses over a set period (usually a financial year).
- The key elements of a Statement of Profit or Loss are:
  - **Revenue:** total income from sales.
  - **Cost of Sales:** direct costs of producing goods/services.
  - **Gross Profit:** Revenue – Cost of Sales.
  - **Expenses:** operating costs such as rent, wages, and marketing.
  - **Net Profit:** final profit after all deductions.

Type of profit	Formula	Tells us...
Gross Profit	Revenue – Cost of Sales	Profit before other expenses
Net Profit	Gross Profit – Expenses	Final profit after all costs

- For example, if Revenue = **£10,000**, Cost of Sales = **£6,000**, and expenses = **£2,500**:
  - Gross Profit = £10,000 – £6,000 = **£4,000**
  - Net Profit = £4,000 – £2,500 = **£1,500**
- **Importance of profit:**
  - **Reward for risk:** entrepreneurs invest time and capital; profit is their return. For example, the Airbnb founders bet on the unproven idea of strangers renting out their homes, but this risk paid off and changed the marketplace of short-term accommodation.
  - **Reinvestment:** enables growth, innovation, and upgrades. For example, the clothing brand AYBL used substantial profits in 2023–2024 to invest in logistics, international warehousing, and supply expansion to support future growth.
  - **Success indicator:** a profitable business attracts investors and improves creditworthiness. For example, a fitness startup uses profits to add new gym equipment and improve its app, enhancing customer experience and long-term growth.
  - **Investor attraction:** investors look for profitable ventures with growth potential. For example, Pret A Manger used its strong profits throughout the 2000s to attract the private equity firm Bridgepoint who acquired a major stake in the company in 2008, facilitating its expansion across Europe and internationally.

Finance

Profit margins and average rate of return (ARR)

Profit margins measure how much profit a business makes as a percentage of its revenue. These help assess financial performance and whether an investment is worthwhile.
- **Profit margins:** higher margins suggest efficient operations and pricing.
  - Gross Profit Margin (%) = (Gross Profit ÷ Revenue) × 100
  - Net Profit Margin (%) = (Net Profit ÷ Revenue) × 100
- **Average rate of return (ARR):** helps a business assess the profitability of an investment over time. It compares the average annual profit from an investment to the initial cost.
  - ARR = (Average Annual Profit ÷ Investment Cost) × 100
- **Example:**
  - Investment = **£10,000**
  - Profit per year = **£2,000 over 5 years**
  - ARR = (£2,000 ÷ £10,000) × 100 = **20%**

Profitability ratios

These ratios assess how efficiently a business converts revenue into profit.

Profitability ratios	Formula	What it shows
Gross Profit Margin	(Gross Profit ÷ Revenue) × 100	Pre-expense profitability
Net Profit Margin	(Net Profit ÷ Revenue) × 100	Final profitability
Return on Capital Employed (ROCE)	(Net Profit ÷ Capital Employed) × 100	Profit earned per £1 invested

Example:
- Net Profit: £25,000
- Capital Employed: £100,000
- ROCE = (25,000 ÷ 100,000) × 100 = **25%**

Statement of financial position (Balance Sheet)

This document shows what the business owns (assets), owes (liabilities), and the capital invested.
- **Components:**

Type	Examples
Non-Current Assets	Land, buildings, machinery
Current Assets	Cash, inventory, trade receivables
Current Liabilities	Overdrafts, trade payables
Non-Current Liabilities	Loans lasting over a year
Capital Employed	Total funding invested in the business

- **Key calculations:**
  - Working Capital = Current Assets − Current Liabilities
  - Total Assets = Current Assets + Non-Current Assets
  - Total Liabilities = Current + Non-Current Liabilities

Liquidity

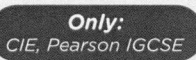

Liquidity measures the ability to cover short-term debts using current assets (i.e. can the business pay its bills?).

Liquidity ratios	Formula	What it shows
Current Ratio	Current Assets ÷ Current Liabilities	General short-term financial health (ideal: 1.5–2)
Acid Test Ratio	(Current Assets − Inventory) ÷ Current Liabilities	Liquidity excluding stock (ideal: above 1)

Example:
- Current Assets = **£30,000**
- Inventory = **£10,000**
- Current Liabilities = **£15,000**
- Current Ratio = £30,000 ÷ £15,000 = **2.0**
- Acid Test Ratio = (£30,000 − £10,000) ÷ £15,000 = **1.33**

Human resources

Function of human resources
- Human resources (HR) is the department or function of a business responsible for managing people – the most valuable asset of any organisation.
- Effective HR management ensures that the business recruits the right people, develops their skills, motivates them, and complies with employment laws.
- HR also includes how businesses structure their workforce, recruit and retain staff, develop talent, and respond to changes in the modern workplace.

Organisational structures
Organisational structures define how roles, responsibilities, and authority are arranged within a business. They help establish clear reporting lines, facilitate communication, and determine decision-making processes. The right structure depends on the size, goals, and culture of the business.

Type	Features	Suitable for
Hierarchical	Clear levels of authority, long chain of command	Larger, traditional organisations
Flat	Fewer layers, wider spans of control	Startups, creative industries, tech firms
Centralised	Decision-making concentrated at the top	Businesses needing consistency or control
Decentralised	Decision-making delegated to lower levels or branches	Multi-site businesses or franchises

- **Tall (hierarchical, centralised) structures** with many levels promote control but can slow decision-making.
- **Flat, decentralised structures** with few levels promote faster communication but can stretch managerial capacity and lead to confusion about responsibilities.
- For example, IKEA uses a hierarchical but decentralised structure, allowing local branches autonomy within a globally consistent framework.

Leadership styles

Only: CIE

Leadership style shapes how decisions are made and how employees are treated. The best style depends on the task, the team, and the business environment.

Style	Characteristics	Advantages	Disadvantages
Autocratic	Manager makes decisions unilaterally	Quick decisions, best in crises or where fast action is needed	Low morale, limited creativity
Democratic	Team is involved in decision-making	High engagement, good ideas, ideal for inclusive/respectful work culture and knowledge-based roles	Can be time-consuming
Laissez-faire	Employees work independently	Encourages innovation, useful in creative sectors	Risk of poor coordination, and requires capable staff

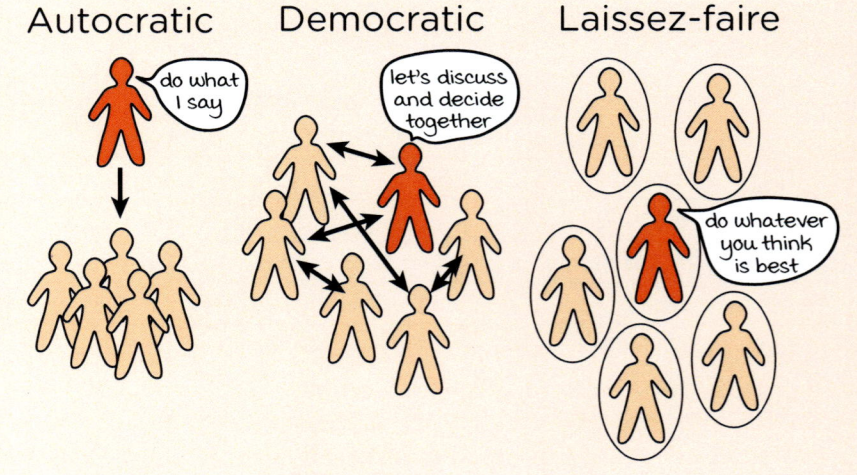

Human resources

Ways of working

In today's dynamic business environment, companies offer a range of working arrangements to meet both **organisational needs** and **employee expectations**. These working patterns help businesses stay agile while promoting work-life balance, employee satisfaction, and access to a wider talent pool.

Advances in **technology**—such as cloud computing, collaborative platforms, and video conferencing—have transformed the way people work. Businesses are no longer limited to local talent or fixed office hours, and employees increasingly expect flexibility and autonomy.

Type of working arrangement	Description	Suitable for
Full-time	Usually 35–40 hours per week, often with regular hours and full employment benefits	Core staff; roles requiring continuity and responsibility
Part-time	Fewer hours than full-time; often used for flexibility or to balance other commitments	Students, parents, carers, or semi-retired workers
Flexible working	Any arrangement that allows variation in working hours, location, or patterns	Employees seeking work-life balance; businesses needing adaptability
Permanent contracts	Ongoing employment with benefits such as holiday pay, pensions, and job security	Long-term positions; roles requiring loyalty and continuity
Temporary contracts	Fixed-term roles, often linked to a time-specific task, event, or peak season	Seasonal roles (e.g. retail during holidays), cover for absences
Freelancers	Self-employed individuals hired to complete specific tasks, usually for short-term work	Creative industries, IT, marketing, writing, design

The impact of technology on working arrangements

Technology has expanded possibilities for how and where people work.

Tool or system	Impact on work
Video conferencing	Enables virtual meetings and interviews across locations (e.g. Zoom, Teams)
Cloud storage	Allows access to shared documents anywhere, anytime (e.g. Google Drive, OneDrive)
Communication platforms	Encourages real-time collaboration and updates (e.g. Slack, Trello, Asana)
Remote desktops and VPNs	Allow employees to securely access company systems from home

Examples:
- **Amazon** hires thousands of temporary workers during the holiday period to manage increased demand in warehouses and customer service.
- **Spotify** introduced a 'Work From Anywhere' policy in 2021, allowing employees to choose whether to work remotely, in the office, or a mix.
- **UK Civil Service** offers compressed hours and job sharing to improve work-life balance and attract a wider talent pool.

	Advantages	Disadvantages
For a business	Greater flexibility and agility	Harder to manage and supervise remote teams
For a business	Access to a global workforce	Communication challenges across time zones
For a business	Reduced office costs	Risk of reduced cohesion or company culture
For employees	Improved work-life balance	Isolation or difficulty separating work/home life
For employees	Choice over when/how to work	Insecurity in temporary/freelance roles
For employees	Good for people who can't work a conventional '9-to-5' office job	Can lead to a lack of work culture or sense of belonging in a business

Human resources

Job roles and responsibilities

A clear organisational structure ensures that everyone in a business understands their duties and reporting lines. This promotes **efficiency**, **accountability**, and **effective decision-making**. Job roles are usually arranged in levels of hierarchy from strategic to operational.

This structure matters because it:
- Ensures clear reporting lines (e.g. staff report to supervisors)
- Avoids duplication of work
- Improves accountability and delegation
- Makes it easier to assess performance at each level

Role	Responsibilities	Examples
Directors	Set the business's overall **strategic vision**, ensure **legal compliance**, make high-level decisions about growth, investment, and risk. Accountable to shareholders (in limited companies).	In Tesco, directors decide national pricing strategy or major expansions like launching a new brand.
Senior managers	Implement the company's strategy within specific **departments** (e.g. marketing, operations). Set departmental goals and manage budgets.	Tesco's regional managers ensure that stores in their area meet sales targets and operate efficiently.
Supervisors/ team leaders	Oversee **day-to-day activities** of staff, provide support, monitor performance, ensure tasks are completed on time.	In a Tesco store, a shift supervisor manages the checkout team during a busy period.
Operational staff	Deliver the core **products or services**—interacting with customers, producing goods, or completing services.	Cashiers and shelf-stackers at Tesco, or baristas at Starbucks.
Support staff	Provide essential **administrative and technical support** (e.g. IT, HR, payroll, finance) to ensure the smooth running of operations.	HR staff at Tesco handle recruitment, training records, and employee benefits.

Effective communication

Effective communication is **the exchange of information** between people in a business. It ensures that **employees understand objectives, expectations, values, and tasks**, which improves performance across the organisation.

- **Barriers to communication:** anything that **disrupts the clarity, accuracy, or flow of information**, causing misunderstandings or inefficiency.
  - **Poor technology or systems:** outdated or incompatible IT can delay messages or lose important data.
  - **Too many management layers:** long chains of command can slow message delivery or distort meaning.
  - **Language and cultural differences:** can lead to misinterpretation, especially in global teams.
  - **Lack of active listening or feedback:** results in people feeling ignored or unclear about next steps.
- **Methods of communication:**

Method	Examples	Advantages	Disadvantages
Verbal (face-to-face or video)	Meetings, feedback, performance reviews	Personal, immediate dialogue	Time-consuming, may not be recorded
Written (emails, memos)	Instructions, updates, reports	Can be reviewed later, easy to share	Risk of being misunderstood
Visual (charts, presentations)	Data sharing, marketing	Clarifies complex info quickly	May need explanation
Digital (apps, intranet)	Remote collaboration	Fast, convenient, widely accessible	Can cause overload if overused

- **Technology and communication:** digital tools have transformed internal and external communication both internally and externally.
  - **Internal:** Slack, Microsoft Teams, Zoom, Google Meet enable fast collaboration, even across time zones.
  - **External:** websites, email marketing, and social media allow for real-time customer updates and feedback.

Human resources

Types of recruitment

Recruitment is the process of **finding and selecting the right candidates** to fill job vacancies. Effective recruitment helps the business maintain a skilled, motivated workforce and achieve long-term success. Recruitment can either be **internal** or **external**.
- **Internal:** promoting or transferring existing staff.
- **External:** recruiting new staff from outside the business.

Type of recruitment	Advantages	Disadvantages
Internal	• Saves time and money • Staff are already familiar with company culture • Motivates employees through career progression	• Limits the pool of applicants • May create jealousy or internal conflict
External	• Access to fresh ideas and new skills • Helps fill skill gaps • Brings in external experience	• More expensive (advertising, agency fees) • Longer process • Training may be required

Effective businesses will typically use a combination of these two types of recruitment. For example, Tesco may use **internal recruitment** to promote a team leader to assistant manager since the desired skills likely already exist within their current pool of staff, whereas they would use **external recruitment** for a specialist IT role that is unlikely to be within the purview of their existing staff.

A good recruitment process ensures **compliance with employment law**, prevents **discrimination**, and promotes **diversity**.

Key recruitment documents

Document	Purpose
Job description	Describes the **main duties**, responsibilities, working hours, and location. This helps candidates understand the role and filter for suitability.
Person specification	Outlines the **skills, qualifications, experience**, and personal qualities needed. This can include essential requirements (e.g. a degree in mathematics) and desirable criteria (e.g. enthusiasm for working in collaborate environments).
Application form/ Curriculum vitae (CV)	Used to **compare candidates** and shortlist for interviews. These provide background on experience, skills, and education, typically listing all past roles, responsibilities, and achievements. Businesses may also request references from one or more most recent employers.
Cover letter	May be required of applicants by a business to **assess suitability** for the role, often including instructions like 'address this to the head of HR' or 'outline why you believe you would be a good fit for our company.' This is slightly more personal than a CV, offering the business a chance to hear from a candidate directly.

Stages in the recruitment process

1. **Identify a vacancy:** triggered by expansion, staff leaving, or new roles being created.
2. **Write the job description and person specification:** ensures the recruitment is focused and transparent.
3. **Advertise the job:** internally (e.g. staff intranet) or externally (e.g. job boards, social media, recruitment agencies).
4. **Receive applications:** candidates apply using a CV or online form.
5. **Shortlist candidates:** applications are reviewed and scored against the person specification.
6. **Interview candidates:** can include multiple rounds, tests, or assessments depending on the role.
7. **Make a job offer and issue a contract:** includes agreeing on salary, start date, and terms and conditions.

Human resources

Employment contracts and legal controls

An **employment contract** is a legal agreement that outlines the rights and duties of employer and employee. Non-compliance with legal controls can lead to fines, legal action, or reputational harm.
- Typical contents of an employment contract are:
  - Job title, duties
  - Pay and working hours
  - Leave entitlements
  - Termination conditions
- Employment law covers:
  - **National minimum wage:** ensures fair pay.
  - **Health and safety:** requires safe working conditions.
  - **Unfair dismissal:** prevents employees being sacked without reason.
  - **Anti-discrimination:** protects from bias against race, gender, age, etc.

Trade unions

Only: CIE, WJEC, Eduqas, CCEA

Trade unions are **organisations that represent the interests of workers**, giving them a collective voice when negotiating with employers. They play an important role in balancing the power between individual employees and large businesses, often at national levels (e.g. education, healthcare).
- **Key roles of trade unions:**
  - **Collective bargaining:** unions negotiate with employers on behalf of members over issues such as pay, working hours, health and safety, and holiday entitlement.
  - **Dispute resolution:** represent employees during workplace disputes, disciplinary hearings, or grievance procedures.
  - **Legal and practical support:** provide legal advice, support during tribunal cases, and representation in unfair dismissal or redundancy situations.
  - **Lobbying and campaigns:** push for changes in employment law or public policy that affect workers' rights (e.g. minimum wage increases, anti-discrimination laws).
- **Trade union membership:** workers voluntarily join and pay a membership fee. Some businesses recognise unions officially, while others do not (non-recognition limits the union's power).

Downsizing and redundancy

Businesses may need to **reduce the size of their workforce** due to financial challenges, strategic shifts, or changes in technology. While these decisions can improve efficiency or cut costs, they must be handled with legal care and sensitivity to employees.
- **Downsizing:** a broad term referring to the **overall reduction in employee numbers**, often as part of a restructuring or cost-cutting strategy. This may include redundancies, early retirements, or not replacing staff who leave. It is aimed at improving **profitability**, **efficiency**, or **survival** in a competitive market.
- **Redundancy:** a specific legal process where a job role is **no longer required**. Redundancy is not about individual performance but about the role itself being eliminated. It is often part of a downsizing strategy.
- **Common causes of downsizing and redundancy:**
  - **Automation:** machines or software replace human roles (e.g. self-service checkouts reducing cashier jobs).
  - **Relocation:** shifting operations to cheaper or more strategic locations (e.g. moving a call centre abroad).
  - **Mergers and acquisitions:** duplicate roles (e.g. two finance departments) may be consolidated.
  - **Falling demand:** when demand for a product or service drops (e.g. DVD rental shops in the streaming era).
- **Legal requirements:** to remain lawful, redundancy must be:
  - **Fair and justified:** based on objective criteria (e.g. role duplication, not personal preference).
  - **Consultative:** employers must consult with affected staff (especially in large-scale redundancies).
  - **Compensated:** statutory redundancy pay is usually due for employees with 2+ years of service. This is calculated based on age, length of service, and weekly pay.

Human resources

Training and development

Training and development refer to the **ongoing process of improving employee skills, knowledge, and performance**. It helps workers stay effective and confident in their roles, especially as businesses face changing technologies and market conditions.

Type of training	Description	Example
Formal training	Delivered through structured programmes, often run by professional trainers or external providers	A customer service team attending a workshop on dealing with complaints
Informal training	Unstructured support provided during daily tasks, such as guidance from a colleague or manager	A new hire learning how to use a point-of-sale system from a co-worker
Self-learning	Independent study through online platforms, reading, or video tutorials	An employee using LinkedIn Learning to develop Excel skills
Ongoing development	Continuous professional development (CPD) over time, aimed at long-term growth	A marketing manager attending annual industry conferences and webinars

- **Benefits of training:**
  - **Improved productivity:** skilled workers are faster and more accurate.
  - **Greater adaptability:** employees can handle new systems or challenges, such as digital transformation or regulatory changes.
  - **Higher morale and motivation:** training shows that a business invests in its people, increasing job satisfaction.
  - **Better staff retention:** workers are less likely to leave if they see career progression opportunities.
  - **Improved quality:** fewer errors or defects due to better-trained staff.
- **Retraining and technology:** as industries adopt **automation, AI, and digital tools**, businesses must **retrain employees** to use new systems. For example, retail staff may need to learn how to manage online orders or digital inventory systems.

Motivation in the workplace

Motivation refers to the **desire and commitment employees have to perform their work well**. A motivated workforce is crucial for achieving business goals and maintaining a competitive edge. Motivation helps:
- **Boosts productivity:** motivated staff work more efficiently and take pride in their output.
- **Reduces absenteeism:** people are less likely to call in sick when they enjoy their work.
- **Improves staff retention:** happy, motivated workers stay with the company longer, reducing recruitment costs.
- **Enhances reputation:** motivated teams often provide better customer service, strengthening brand loyalty.
- **Attracts skilled talent:** a reputation for employee satisfaction draws strong candidates.

	Method of motivation	Description	Example
Financial methods	Wages and salaries	Regular pay incentivises consistent performance	Retail workers on an hourly wage
Financial methods	Bonuses and commission	Extra pay based on performance or sales targets	A car salesperson receiving commission per vehicle sold
Financial methods	Fringe benefits	Non-cash perks such as a company car or gym membership	Tech firms offering staff free meals and wellness benefits
Financial methods	Promotions	Advancing to a higher role with greater pay and responsibility	An assistant manager being promoted to store manager
Non-financial methods	Job enrichment	Giving employees more responsibility or meaningful tasks	A chef designing new menu items, not just preparing food
Non-financial methods	Autonomy	Letting employees make decisions and manage their own work	A graphic designer choosing how to approach a campaign
Non-financial methods	Job rotation	Moving employees between different tasks or roles to prevent boredom	A factory worker switching between picking and packing
Non-financial methods	Recognition	Public praise, awards, or certificates for good performance.	'Employee of the Month' schemes or shout-outs in team meetings.

Formula sheet

Concept	Formula
Total costs	TC = TFC + TVC (total cost) (total fixed cost) (total variable cost)
Revenue	revenue = price × quantity
Gross profit	gross profit = sales revenue − cost of sales
Gross profit margin	gross profit margin (%) = $\frac{\text{gross profit}}{\text{sales revenue}} \times 100$
Net profit	net profit = gross profit − other operating expenses and interest
Net profit margin	net profit margin (%) = $\frac{\text{net profit}}{\text{sales return}} \times 100$
Average rate of return	rate of return = $\frac{\text{average annual profit}}{\text{cost of investment}} \times 100$
Net cash flow	net cash flow = cash inflows − cash outflows (in a given period)
Break even point	break even point = $\frac{\text{fixed cost}}{\text{sales price} - \text{variable cost}}$
Margin of safety	margin = actual or budgeted sales − break even sales

Concept	Formula
Interest on loans	interest (%) = $\frac{\text{total repayment} - \text{borrowed amount}}{\text{borrowed amount}} \times 100$
Opening and closing balance	opening balance = closing balance of previous period closing balance = opening balance + net cash flow
Market share	market share = $\frac{\text{sales revenue of a business}}{\text{total sales revenue for the market}} \times 100$
Labour productivity	units per employee = $\frac{\text{output per period (units)}}{\text{number of employees}}$
Working capital	working capital = current assets − current liabilities
Return on capital employed (ROCE)	ROCE = $\frac{\text{profit}}{\text{capital employed}} \times 100$
Current liquidity ratio *Only: CIE*	current assets : current liabilities
Acid test ratio *Only: CIE*	current assets − inventory : current liabilities